LOUIS EUGÈNE BOUDIN
Precursor of Impressionism

LOUIS EUGÈNE BOUDIN

Precursor of Impressionism

An exhibition organized by
Mahonri Sharp Young and Katherine Wallace Paris

Santa Barbara Museum of Art
Santa Barbara California
October 8 to November 21, 1976

Museum of Fine Arts
St. Petersburg Florida
January 18 to February 27, 1977

Art Museum of South Texas
Corpus Christi Texas
December 2, 1976 to January 9, 1977

Columbus Gallery of Fine Arts
Columbus Ohio
March 10 to April 24, 1977

Fine Arts Gallery of San Diego
San Diego California
May 5 to June 12, 1977

Copyright © 1976 Santa Barbara Museum of Art
Library of Congress Catalogue Number 76-4538

1750 copies of this catalogue have been printed by
The Watkins Printing Company

Designer: Harold M. Stevens

This project is supported by a grant from the National Endowment for the Arts in Washington, D.C., a Federal agency.

ACKNOWLEDGMENTS

Many individuals as well as organizations have helped in the preparation of this exhibition and the accompanying catalog; we extend our sincere gratitude and appreciation to all of them. It would not be possible to name each one, but we would like to extend our special thanks to Robert Schmit, author of the catalogue raisonné (*Eugène Boudin*, *1824–1898*, Paris, 1973) for his kind permission to translate some of those materials for inclusion here.

To the collectors and museums, listed separately, who have so generously shared their pictures with us, and the National Endowment for the Arts whose generous matching grant supported the exhibition and catalog, our thanks for making exhibitions of this kind possible.

Our thanks also to the staffs of the Frick Art Reference Library and the New York Public Library for their never-failing courteous service, and to Norman Hirschl and Stephen Hahn.

We would like to express appreciation to the staff of the Santa Barbara Museum of Art and particularly to Paul Mills, director; Richard Kubiak, curator of exhibitions; and Terrell Hillebrand, registrar. To the staff of our own museum, The Columbus Gallery of Fine Arts, we offer a special note of thanks for their unceasing enthusiasm and hard work on the project, particularly: Catherine Clader Glasgow, research assistant; Kathleen MacLean and Linda Gentis Larrimer, research aids; Betty Rosbottom and Ann Daniels, departmental assistants; and Pat Reed for her help.

Katherine Wallace Paris

LENDERS TO THE EXHIBITION

Albright-Knox Art Gallery, Buffalo, New York
Anonymous Lenders
Mr. & Mrs. Robert E. Blum
The Cleveland Museum of Art, Ohio
Mr. & Mrs. Jan de Graaff
Mrs. Chauncey B. Garver
Stephen Hahn Gallery, New York
Art Gallery of Hamilton, Ontario, Canada
The High Museum of Art, Atlanta, Georgia
Hirschl & Adler Galleries, New York
Mr. & Mrs. David Lloyd Kreeger
Los Angeles County Museum of Art, California
Marion Koogler McNay Art Institute, San Antonio, Texas
The Metropolitan Museum of Art, New York
The University of Michigan Museum of Art, Ann Arbor

The Montreal Museum of Fine Arts, Quebec, Canada
Mr. & Mrs. Irving Moskovitz
The Philadelphia Museum of Art, Pennsylvania
The Phillips Collection, Washington, D.C.
The Art Museum, Princeton University, New Jersey
Musée du Québec, Canada
Everett D. Reese
Museum of Art, Rhode Island School of Design, Providence
John & Mable Ringling Museum of Art, Sarasota, Florida
Peter A. Salm
Fine Arts Gallery of San Diego, California
The Fine Arts Museum of San Francisco, California
Santa Barbara Museum of Art, California
Dr. & Mrs. Abraham Schlossman
Mr. & Mrs. Benjamin Victor
Wildenstein & Company, New York

FOREWORD

It will come as a matter of some surprise that this is the first one-man exhibition in forty years, organized by a museum in this country, dedicated to the work of Eugène Boudin. To anyone whose acquaintance with the arts extends to the borders of the territory of the Impressionists, he is well-known: he is thought of as the link between the Barbizon School and the Impressionists; he is known as the friend of the artists who painted at Le Havre and along the north coast; and he is especially remembered as the early mentor of Monet. He is not merely a name; his modest yet ravishing little views of harbors and ships and beaches and clouds are sought after by collectors who are better known for their acquisition of works by Impressionist masters. His essays on sea and ship and sky, depicted in a reserved but sumptuous pearl-grey palette, outshine many more celebrated works. It is not too surprising that the trustees of the National Gallery of Art, who could have selected the works of other more celebrated artists to adorn their boardroom, have chosen to hang there a splendid collection of Boudins for their personal delection.

This exhibition, as it happens, marks other events. It has to do with old men and young men, which I feel would have pleased Boudin. It all came about because my first museum job, at the Henry Gallery of the University of Washington many years ago, involved my working on the Barbizon collection assembled by the Henrys and developed in me a special attachment to a beautiful little Boudin, which I hung over my desk anytime it was not on display in the galleries. It also led me to do an undergraduate thesis on his work. Here in Santa Barbara, seeing the many handsome paintings in the collection of Mrs. L. H. Kirkpatrick, I must admit I positively pounced upon a most unusual Boudin view of the cathedral at Abbeville and she, some time after, generously presented it to the museum. To celebrate this acquisition and to redirect a little of our national attention from the Impressionist stars to an artist both deserving and rewarding, we proposed a Boudin exhibition. Happily, the National Endowment for the Arts concurred — one more sign in my mind of the special wisdom it brings to its role in the arts in this country.

It could not be more appropriate that this exhibition was assembled by Mahonri Sharp Young, most knowing and articulate of the American friends of Boudin. There is also a bit of poetic justice of some sort occurring: as this exhibition stemmed from my very first assignment as a museum professional, over a quarter of a century ago; so it is the last assignment for Bill Young as director of the Columbus Gallery of Fine Arts, from which he is retiring after twenty-three years. Fortunately, he will continue to be the American correspondent for *Apollo Magazine*, whose pages regularly present his comments on the arts in this country in that distinctive style of his which manages to be at once both iconoclastic and civilized.

Our warmest thanks to him and to his staff. Our special thanks to the lenders to this exhibition who are, in fact, truly the ones who have made it possible at all. Their willingness to share these pleasures with others is much to be commended! And now we invite you to enjoy what surely is one of the finest little feasts of art held in many years.

Paul C. Mills, director
Santa Barbara Museum of Art
July 21, 1976

BOUDIN: A Precursor of Impressionism

Although Boudin is far from a neglected artist, this is his first museum show in four decades. An important and delightful painter, Boudin played a major part in the rise of Impressionism and he's a charmer in his own right. His painting came out of the Forest of Fontainebleau, and Corot is the man behind Boudin's skies and his light. But Monet, who *is* Impressionism, comes straight out of Boudin.

Boudin was born in Normandy and lived in that part of France all his life. For a sea painter, it was perfect; his Dutch friend Jongkind, a sea painter from the same mold, said it was where he would like to live. Though Boudin's father was a deckhand and his mother a stewardess, his own maritime career was short: when he was ten, he fell off his father's boat, on which he was serving as a cabin boy, and that was the end. After his family moved to Le Havre from Honfleur, no great journey, young Boudin went to work in a stationery store; when his boss saw the boy drawing, he gave him a box of paints.

Later, in his own shop, Boudin sold pictures by Troyon and Isabey. When Millet, who was having a hell of a time, found that the young businessman wanted to become an artist, he told him an artist's life is not fit for a dog. When his number came up in the draft, Boudin had to pull his capital out of the firm to pay a substitute. From then on he was on his own; he had a pretty thin time, but he had the great advantage of doing exactly what he wanted, which is not what you do in a stationery store.

In many ways it was a very good life. He was always poor, but so are most people. He loved his work, he knew it was good, and the other artists knew it; those are the important things. You can make a good case for Boudin's life; his work was what he hoped it was. The tragedy is when the artist takes all the risks, and the work is no good. If you have Boudin's sense of discovery and delight you are a happy man. We see exactly what he saw, and we feel exactly what he felt.

As for Monet's debt, there isn't any question:

"I remember our meeting as if it were yesterday. I was in the framer's shop where I often exhibited the pencil caricatures which had won me some notoriety in Le Havre, and even a little money. I met Eugène Boudin there. He was then about thirty, and his expansive and generous personality were already apparent. [In fact, Boudin was thirty-five, and Monet eighteen.] I had seen his work on several occasions, and I must admit I thought it was frightful. 'These little things are yours, are they, young man?' he asked. 'It's a pity you don't aim higher, for you obviously have talent. Why don't you paint?'

"I confess that the thought of painting in Boudin's idiom didn't exactly thrill me. But, when he insisted, I agreed to go painting in the open air with him. I bought a paint box, and we set off to Rouelles, without much enthusiasm on my part. I watched him rather apprehensively, and then more attentively, and then suddenly it was as if a veil had been torn from my eyes. I had understood, I had grasped what painting could be. Boudin's absorption in his work, and his independence, were enough to decide the entire future and development of my painting." (*Eugène Boudin* by G. Jean-Aubry with Robert Schmit, Greenwich, Connecticut, 1968, pp.

24–25.) As Monet said on at least two occasions, "If I have become a painter, I owe it to Eugène Boudin."

This laying-on of hands probably occurred in 1858. The next year, Courbet became a friend; one day they had dinner with Baudelaire and his mother, and Baudelaire was so pleased with the company that he went all the way back to Paris with them; Baudelaire hated the country when the weather was good because it was too much like India. Courbet said Boudin must be an angel, because he knew what the sky was really like. Baudelaire could review the Salon without seeing it, but he was very familiar with Boudin's studies, "so quickly and so faithfully sketched from the elements in nature which are the most inconstant and elusive in form and color; waves and clouds," and Baudelaire was sure that "in time to come he will capture the magic of air and water in finished works as well as sketches." That is exactly what he has done in this splendid batch of pictures which will bring the beauty of the Normandy beaches to Santa Barbara, Corpus Christi, St. Petersburg, San Diego and Columbus.

I would like to thank Paul Mills for asking me to do the show, and Katherine Paris for doing so much of the work.

Mahonri Sharp Young

BIOGRAPHY

1824   Louis Eugène Boudin was born on July 12 at Honfleur to a modest family.

1834   At the age of 10, Boudin set off as a deckboy on his father's small boat, *Le Polichinelle*.

1835   The family settled at Le Havre. Boudin began work as a salesman in the stationer's shop of Alphonse Lemasle, where he remained for 18 years. There he befriended a fellow employee named Jean Archer.

1844   Together they established a stationer's shop and Boudin came to know Isabey, Troyon, Couture, and Millet, whose works he often displayed in his shop window.

1846   Boudin's passion for painting became irresistible. He sold his share of the business to buy a replacement to do his military service and avoid enlistment, allowing him to devote himself entirely to his art.

1847   Boudin left for Paris.

1848   He accompanied the sculptor Rochet on a journey to Belgium and was able to study the works of the old Flemish Masters.

1851   He was awarded a grant from the town of Le Havre, which he used to work in the Honfleur district.

1853   He began a notebook, an accounting of the struggle of a young artist to survive the hardships, indecision, and fears peculiar to his trade. Boudin continued to work furiously, exhibited on occasion, and made a sale or two.

1858   This is very probably the year in which Boudin met Claude Monet.

1859   Despite Monet's wish that he come to Paris, Boudin remained at Le Havre. He met Baudelaire and began a friendship with Courbet that never faltered. For the first time, one of his canvases was shown in the Salon of Paris. He then decided to settle permanently in Paris and established a studio on the Boulevard Montmartre. He worked closely with Troyon and tried unsuccessfully to sell his paintings.

1860   He traveled to Honfleur, Trouville, and to Quimper.

1861   Boudin met Corot and Daubigny.

1862   He traveled to Trouville where he met Jongkind, a friend of Monet. Following the advice of Isabey, he began to paint beach scenes.

1863   In January he married. Each summer he returned to the sea: Le Havre, Trouville, Deauville.

1864   The winter in Paris was encouraging. Boudin began to seriously establish his reputation.

1866   He was noticed by the critics.

1867   Each summer, he continued to return to the sea, Brittany or Normandy, painting beaches, markets, or religious festivals.

1868   Boudin participated in an important exhibition at Le Havre with Courbet, Manet, Monet, and Daubigny.

1869   A few dealers commissioned canvases and Boudin began to enjoy the beginnings of success.

1870   The war forced him to flee to Brussels.

1871   Boudin returned to Paris to find his reputation and patrons growing. Over the following years, he traveled extensively in Normandy, Brittany, and Bordeaux; to Berck, in the Netherlands; and Beaulieu.

1881   Monsieur Durand-Ruel began organizing an exhibition of Boudin's work to inaugurate his new premises on the Boulevard de la Madeleine.

1883   This exhibition at Durand-Ruel was so well received by the press and the collectors that it firmly established Eugène Boudin as an artist of the highest standing. Durand-Ruel, impressed by the requests of the buyers, retrieved all of the paintings scattered among his colleagues in order to become Boudin's exclusive dealer.

1884 He traveled to Dordrecht, and then to Trouville, the district he preferred.

1886 The State purchased one of his paintings from the Salon.

1888 Again, the State purchased one of his paintings from the Salon.

1889 He painted pastoral scenes of cows grazing along the banks of the Touques River.

1890 He joined the "Societé des Beaux-Arts," founded by the dissenters of the Salon, of which Meissonier was the president. Durand-Ruel gave him an exhibition in Paris.

1891 Boudin traveled to Etaples, a visit that produced a fine series of paintings. Durand-Ruel organized another one-man exhibition for him in Paris. Finally the "Golden Age" of the French painter had arrived, and Boudin was an important part of it.

1892 Stricken with a painful nerve disease, Boudin was forced to spend his winters in a milder climate. He began a regular journey to Antibes, Villefranche, and Beaulieu and visited Venice for the first time. The State purchased one of his paintings from the Salon and he was awarded the Cross of the Legion of Honor.

1893 He continued to divide his time between his studio in Paris, his villa in Deauville, and the South of France.

1895 Tired and growing old, Boudin nevertheless continued to paint with enthusiasm, traveling again to all of those places along the coast that he had known so well: Honfleur, Le Havre, Trouville, Deauville, Dieppe, Étretat.

1898 Boudin left Paris one last time for Beaulieu with the delusive hope of improving his health; but, suffering from cancer of the stomach, he grew weaker again, left with no more than an eagerness to return to his dear Normandy. He devoted himself to the cataloguing of his paintings and drawings, and to determining how they would be distributed after his death.

Boudin was brought back to Deauville, to his home facing the sea, where he died August 8.

BOUDIN: Where and When He Painted

Abbeville: 1890, 1894

Antibes: 1892–1893, 1897

Anvers: 1870–1875, 1880, 1886 (principally 1871)

Argenteuil: 1866

Beaulieu: 1892–1893, 1898 (here he painted his last canvas)

Bénerville: 1890, 1893, 1897

Bénodet: 1872

Berck: 1870–1895 (principally 1875, 1881–1882, 1890)

Bergues: 1889

Binic: 1872–1873

Bordeaux: 1870, 1873–1877, 1879 (longest visit in 1874)

Boulogne: 1891

Brest: 1870, 1872–1874, 1879, 1883, 1893 (principally 1872)

Camaret: 1871–1873, 1878 (principally 1873)

Camphroux: 1873

Caudebec-en-Caux: 1889–1890 (principally 1892)

Cayeux: 1890

Oisème (near Chartres): 1888, 1890–1891, 1893

Cherbourg: 1883

Le Croisic: 1897

Le Crotoy: 1890

Deauville: Beach Scenes 1863–1873, Seascapes 1873–1897 (frequent visits 1890 & 1897)

Dieppe: Beach Scenes 1868, Seascapes 1882, 1886, 1888 (principally 1896)

Dordrecht: 1870, 1875–1876, 1880–1881, 1883 (principally 1884, 1885, 1888, 1892)

Doualas (Finistère): 1872

Douarenez: 1855, 1887, 1891 (principally 1897)

Dunkerque: 1870, 1888–1892 (principally 1889)

Elnery (Orne): 1893

Etaples: 1870, 1873, 1880, 1895 (principally 1890)

Etretat: 1883, 1888–1896 (principally 1890)

Le Faou: 1865, 1873–1875

Fécamp: 1872–1874, 1880–1894 (principally 1892)

Fervaques: 1870–1898

Le Havre: Throughout his life but principally 1892–1894

Hennequeville: 1890, 1893

Honfleur: Throughout his life beginning 1850

Juan-les-Pins: 1893, 1895

Kerhor: 1870–1871

Landerneau: 1867–1873, 1897

Lannion: 1871

Nice: 1892

Plougastel: 1870–1876 (principally 1870)

Pont-Aven: 1897

Portrieux: 1869–1874 (principally 1873)

Quiberon: 1893, 1897

Quillebeuf: 1874, 1893

Quimper: 1857

Rotterdam: 1870, 1873–1876, 1879–1880, 1888 (principally 1876)

Rouen: 1895

Saint-Cènery (Orne): 1892

Saint-Valéry: 1886, 1889–1894 (principally 1890)

Saint-Vaast-la-Hougue: 1888, 1892–1893 (principally 1892)

Scheveningue: 1875–1876, 1890

La Touques: 1879–1897

Tourgeville: 1887–1893

Le Tréport: 1880

Trouville: Beach Scenes from 1860, Port Scenes 1885–1898

Venice: 1892–1895 (principally 1895)

Veules: Beach Scenes 1864

Villefranche: 1885, 1890–1894 (principally 1892)

Villers-sur-Mer: 1894–1895

Villerville: 1884, 1893–1896

Vimont: 1875

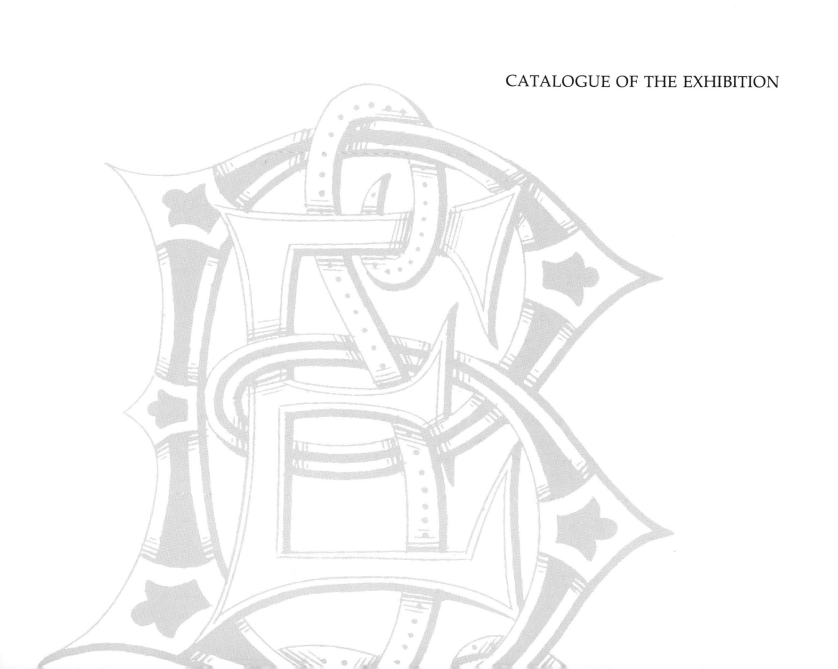

CATALOGUE OF THE EXHIBITION

1. *Nature Morte au Homard sur une Nappe Blanche.* ca. 1862
   (Still Life with Lobster on a White Cloth)

   Oil on canvas
   22½ x 32¼ in. (57.1 x 81.9 cm.)
   Signed lower right: *E. Boudin*
   S.57
   The High Museum of Art, Atlanta, Georgia: Gift in
   memory of Lena B. Jacobs, 1970

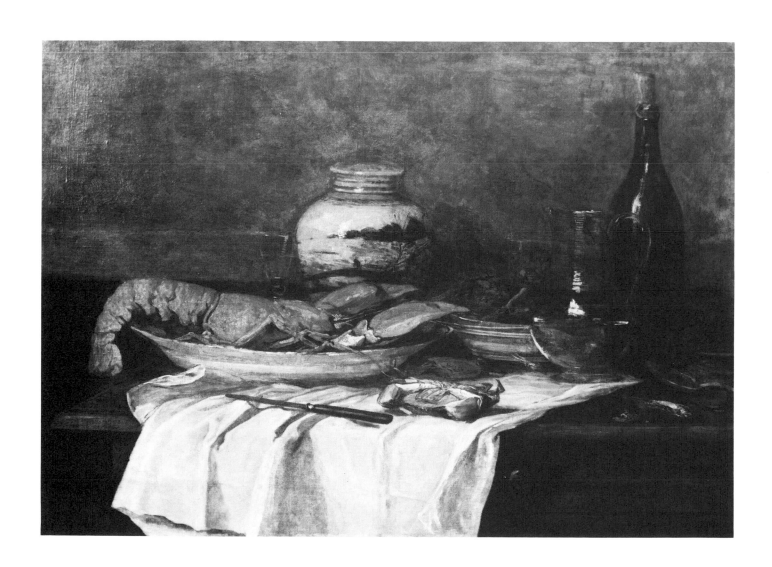

2. *The Beach at Trouville.* 1865

Oil on canvas
15 x 24½ in. (38 x 62.8 cm.)
Signed and dated lower right: *E. Boudin – 65*
S.347 (*Trouville. Scène de Plage*)
The Art Museum, Princeton University, New Jersey

3. *Halage de Bateau.* ca. 1865–1867
   (Hauling the Boat)

   24 x 37 in. (61 x 94 cm.)
   Initialed lower right: *E.B.*
   S.353
   Private Collection

4. *Toulinguet.* 1872

Oil on canvas
21¼ x 35½ in. (53.7 x 90.2 cm.)
Inscribed, dated and signed lower right: *Toulinguet/ 72.
E. Boudin*
S.807 (*Camaret. Le Toulinguet*)
Mr. & Mrs. Benjamin Victor

5. *Vue de Paimpol.* 1872
   (View of Paimpol)

   Oil on canvas
   22 x 41½ in. (55.9 x 105.4 cm.)
   Signed and dated lower left: *E. Boudin 72*
   Inscribed lower right: *Paimpol*
   S.816
   Peter A. Salm

6. *Bordeaux. Le Port.* 1874–1876
   (The Harbor at Bordeaux)

   Oil on canvas
   12½ x 18¼ in. (31.7 x 46.3 cm.)
   Signed lower left: *E. Boudin*
   S.1010
   Hirschl & Adler Galleries, New York

7. *Le Marché aux Poissons à Rotterdam.* ca. 1874–1876
   (The Fish Market at Rotterdam)

   Oil on panel
   15¾ x 21⅝ in. (40 x 54.6 cm.)
   Signed and inscribed lower right: *E. Boudin. Rotterdam*
   S.1029
   Private Collection

8. *Les Dunes de Tourgeville.* 1880
   (The Dunes of Tourgeville)

   Oil on canvas
   15⅞ x 21⁵/₁₆ in. (40.3 x 54.1 cm.)
   Signed and dated lower left: *E. Boudin – 80*
   S.1314
   The Montreal Museum of Fine Arts, Quebec, Canada:
   Presented by Mrs. George R. Robertson in memory of
   her son, 1920

9. *Dunkerque. Les Quais.* 1880
   (The Wharf at Dunkerque)

   Oil on canvas
   16½ x 21½ in. (41.2 x 55.4 cm.)
   Dated and signed lower right: *80/ E Boudin*
   S.2563
   John & Mable Ringling Museum of Art, Sarasota, Florida

10. *Trouville. Scène de Plage.* 1880
    (Beach Scene at Trouville)

    Oil on panel
    7 x 13½ in. (17.8 x 34.3 cm.)
    Signed lower left: *E. Boudin*
    Inscribed and dated lower right: *Trouville 80*
    S.1296
    The Philadelphia Museum of Art, Pennsylvania: Bequest
    of Lisa Norris Elkins

11. *On the River Meuse.* ca. 1882–1883

Oil on canvas
19⅝ x 29¼ in. (49.8 x 74.3 cm.)
Signed lower left: *E. Boudin.*
S.1695 (*Bateaux sur la Meuse*)
The Fine Arts Museums of San Francisco, California: Gift
of H.K.S. Williams to the Mildred Anna Williams Collection

12. *Sur la Meuse.* 1883
    (On the River Meuse)

    Oil on canvas
    21½ x 28⅞ in. (54.5 x 73.5 cm.)
    Signed and dated lower left: *E. Boudin 83*
    S.1744
    Mr. & Mrs. David Lloyd Kreeger

13. *Landscape (Fervaques)*. 1884

Oil on canvas
20 x 27¾ in. (50.8 x 70.7 cm.)
Signed and dated lower left: *E. Boudin – 84*
Inscribed lower right: *Fervaques*
S.1890 (*Fervaques. Pâturage. Au Fond le Village*)
The High Museum of Art, Atlanta, Georgia: J. J. Haverty
Collection

14. *Trouville. Le Marché aux Poissons.* 1884
(The Fish Market at Trouville)

Oil on panel
14¾ x 18⅛ in. (37 x 45 cm.)
Dated and signed lower left: *– 84 – E. Boudin.*
Inscribed lower right: *Trouville*
S.1877
Stephen Hahn Gallery, New York

15. *Trouville. Le Port.* 1884
    (The Harbor at Trouville)

    Oil on board
    9¼ x 12¾ in. (23.3 x 32.7 cm.)
    Signed lower left: *E. Boudin*
    Inscribed and dated lower right: *Trouville 84*
    S.1893
    Art Gallery of Hamilton, Ontario, Canada: Bequest of
    Miss Muriel Bostwick, 1966

16. *Le Grain.* 1885
(The Squall)

Oil on canvas
25¹¹/₁₆ x 35⁹/₁₆ in. (65.2 x 90.3 cm.)
Signed and dated lower right: *E. Boudin 1885*
S.1929 (*Mer Agitée par Temps d'Orage*)
The Montreal Museum of Fine Arts, Quebec, Canada:
Bequest of Dr. F. J. Shepherd, 1929

17. *Marée Basse.* 1885
    (Low Tide)

    Oil on canvas
    26 x 36 in. (66 x 94 cm.)
    Signed and dated lower left: *E. Boudin. 85.*
    Mr. & Mrs. Jan de Graaff

18. *Port de Trouville.* 1885
    (The Port of Trouville)

    Oil on panel
    13½ x 10 in. (34.3 x 25.4 cm.)
    Signed and dated lower left: *E. Boudin – 85*
    S.1922 (*Trouville. Le Port*)
    Los Angeles County Museum of Art, California: Gift of
    Cary Grant

19. *Trouville.* 1886

Oil on canvas
18 x 25½ in. (45.7 x 64.8 cm.)
Signed and dated lower right: *E. Boudin 86.*
S.2175 (*Trouville. Le Port*)
Mr. & Mrs. Robert E. Blum

20. *Le Marché.* 1888–1895
    (The Market)

    Oil on panel
    6⅝ x 7¾ in. (15.9 x 18.5 cm.)
    Signed lower left: *E. Boudin.*
    S.2412 (*Marché* [*Esquisse*])
    Dr. & Mrs. Abraham Schlossman

21. *Pâturage au Bord de la Touques.* ca.1888–1895
    (Landscape along the Touques)

    Oil on canvas
    12⅝ x 18⅛ in. (32 x 46 cm.)
    Signed lower left: *E. Boudin*
    S.2495
    The University of Michigan Museum of Art, Ann Arbor:
    Gift of Dr. & Mrs. Edgar A. Kahn

22. *La Touques. Marée Basse.* ca. 1888–1895
    (The Touques at Low Tide)
    Oil on panel
    16½ x 24 in. (41.9 x 61 cm.)
    Signed lower left: *E. Boudin*
    S.2475
    Private Collection, London

23. *Le Bassin de Deauville*. 1889
(The Dock at Deauville)

Oil on canvas
16⅛ x 21⅝ in. (41 x 55 cm.)
Inscribed, signed and dated lower left: *à son ami/ F. Vinton
E. Boudin 89.*
S.2549 (*Trouville. Le Port*)
Museum of Art, Rhode Island School of Design, Providence: Museum Appropriation

24. *Étretat* 1890

Oil on canvas
16⅛ x 21⅝ in. (41 x 54.9 cm.)
Signed and dated lower right: *E. Boudin 90*
Inscribed lower left: *Étretat*
S.2741 (*Étretat. Barques Echouées sur la Plage et Falaise d'Amont*)
Fine Arts Gallery of San Diego, California: Gift of John F. Kraushaar, 1926

25. *Le Marché à Trouville.* 1890
    (The Market at Trouville)

    Oil on panel
    9⅛ x 13 in. (23.2 x 33 cm.)
    Signed and dated lower right: *E. Boudin – 1890*
    Inscribed lower right: *Trouville*
    S.2692
    The Montreal Museum of Fine Arts, Quebec, Canada:
    Gift of Mrs. John E. Gatehouse, 1933

26. *Le Rivage d'Étretat (Brouillard)*. 1890
   (The Beach at Etretat in the Fog)

   Oil on canvas
   17¾ x 25⅝ in. (45 x 65 cm.)
   Signed, dated and inscribed lower right: *E. Boudin 90./*
   Etretat/ Barques de Sardiniers
   S.2744
   Stephen Hahn Gallery, New York

27. *Deauville Harbor.* 1891

Oil on panel
18 x 15 in. (45.7 x 38.1 cm.)
Signed and dated lower right: *E. Boudin/ 91*
Inscribed lower right: *Deauville.*
S.2833 (*Deauville. Le Bassin*)
The Cleveland Museum of Art, Ohio: Gift of Leonard C.
Hanna, Jr., for the Coralie Walker Hanna Memorial Collection

28. *Le Port de Trouville.* 1891
    (The Harbor of Trouville)

    Oil on panel
    10¾ x 8½ in. (27 x 21.4 cm.)

    Inscribed, signed and dated lower left: *Trouville/E. Boudin 91.*
    Musée du Québec, Canada

29. *Sur la Plage près de Trouville.* 1891
    (On the Beach near Trouville)

    Oil on canvas
    14¾ x 23¼ in. (37.5 x 59 cm.)
    Signed and dated lower right: *E. Boudin 91*
    Private Collection

30. *Beaulieu – The Bay of Fourmis.* 1892

Oil on canvas
21⅝ x 35½ in. (54.6 x 90.2 cm.)
Inscribed, signed and dated lower left: *Beaulieu-Mars/ E.
Boudin. 92*
S.2885 (*Beaulieu. La Baie des Fourmis*)
The Metropolitan Museum of Art, New York: Bequest of
Jacob Ruppert, 1939

31. *Trouville. Les Jetées.* 1892
(The Piers at Trouville)

Oil on panel
14¾ x 18⅛ in. (37.5 x 59 cm.)
Signed and dated lower left: *E. Boudin – 92*
S.2969 (*Trouville. Les Jetées. Marée Haute*)
The Montreal Museum of Fine Arts, Quebec, Canada:
Bequest of John W. Tempest, 1915

32. *Antibes. Vue prise de la Salis.* 1893
(Antibes. View from la Salis)

Oil on canvas
19⅝ x 29⅛ in. (50 x 74 cm.)
Inscribed, signed and dated lower left: *Antibes./ E. Boudin
93.*
S.3100
Wildenstein & Company, New York

33. *Cap d'Antibes.* 1893
    (Cape of Antibes)

    Oil on canvas
    19⅝ x 29⅛ in. (50 x 74 cm.)
    Inscribed, signed and dated lower right: *Antibes/ E.
    Boudin 93*
    S.3092 (*Antibes. Les Rochers de L'Ilette et les Fortifications*)
    Everett D. Reese

34. *The Touques at High Tide.* 1893

Oil on canvas
10¼ x 16 in. (25.4 x 40.6 cm.)
Signed and dated lower right: *E. Boudin 93*
S.3188 *(Les Bords de la Touques)*
Mr. & Mrs. Irving Moskovitz

35. *Cathedral at Abbeville.* 1894

Oil on panel
18 x 14½ in. (45.7 x 36.8 cm.)
Signed and dated lower left: *E. Boudin 94*
Inscribed lower right: *Abbeville*
Santa Barbara Museum of Art, California: Gift of Mrs. L.
H. Kirkpatrick

36. *La Plage de Deauville à marée haute.* 1894
(The Beach of Deauville at High Tide)

Oil on canvas
21⅝ x 31½ in. (55 x 80 cm.)
Inscribed, signed and dated lower left: *Deauville/ E. Boudin 94 Octobre*
S. 3320 (*Deauville. La Plage à Marée Montante*)
Musée du Québec, Canada

37. *Harbour Scene*. 1895
   Oil on canvas
   22¼ x 13½ in. (57.1 x 34.3 cm.)
   Signed and dated lower right: *E. Boudin 95*
   Mrs. Chauncey B. Garver

38. *The Seine at Rouen.* 1895

Oil on canvas
18¼ x 25¾ in. (46.5 x 65.5 cm.)
Inscribed, signed and dated lower left: *Rouen/ E. Boudin 95.*
S.458 (*Rouen. La Seine et la Côte Ste-Catherine*)
Albright-Knox Art Gallery, Buffalo, New York: Gift of Mr. & Mrs. Alfred G. Lewis in memory of Mr. & Mrs. George Howard Lewis

39. *Venise. Le Quai des Esclavons, La Salute.* 1895
    (Venice. The Quai des Esclavons, La Salute.)

    Oil on canvas
    18½ x 25¾ in. (47 x 65.4 cm.)
    Inscribed, signed and dated lower right: *Venise/ E. Boudin 95*
    S.3416 (*Venise. Le Quai des Esclavons, La Salute./ Entrée du Grand Canal/ Fin de Journée* [Titre au Dos])

    The Phillips Collection, Washington, D.C.

40. *Venise. Le Quai des Esclavons le Soir, La Douane et La Salute.* 1895
(Venice. The Quai des Esclavons in the Evening, The Bureau of Customs and La Salute)

Oil on canvas
18⅛ x 25⅝ in. (46 x 65 cm.)
Inscribed, signed and dated lower right: *Venise/ E. Boudin 95*
S.3417
Musée du Québec, Canada

41. *Trouville.* 1896

Oil on canvas
14⅝ x 22¾ in. (37 x 58 cm.)
Inscribed, signed and dated lower left: *Trouville/ E. Boudin 96*
S.3579 *(Trouville. Le Port. Marée Basse)*
Musée du Québec, Canada

42. *Figures on a Beach.* n.d.

Watercolor and pencil on paper
5 x 10½ in. (12.7 x 26.7 cm.) (sight)
Undeciphered pencil marks lower left
Marion Koogler McNay Art Institute, San Antonio,
Texas: Bequest of Marion Koogler McNay

BIBLIOGRAPHY

I. MONOGRAPHS

Arsène Alexandre, *L'œuvre d'Eugène Boudin,* Paris, 1899

Gustave Cahen, *Eugène Boudin, sa vie, son œuvre.* Preface by Arsène Alexandre, Floury, Paris, 1900

G. Jean-Aubry, *Eugène Boudin d'après des documents inédits,* Bernheim-Jeune, Paris, 1922

Claude Roger-Marx, *Eugène Boudin,* Crès, Paris, 1927

Louis Cario, *Eugéne Boudin,* Rieder, Paris, 1928

Ruth L. Benjamin, *Eugene Boudin,* Raymond & Raymond, New York, 1937

Jose Roberto Teixeira Leite, *Boudin no Brasil,* Rio de Janeiro, 1961

G. Jean-Aubry, *Eugène Boudin, la vie et l'œuvre d'après les lettres et les documents inédits,* Ides & Calendes, Neuchâtel, 1968

Robert Schmit, *Eugène Boudin, 1824–1898,* Paris, 1973

II. CATALOGUES

Atelier Eugène Boudin. Catalogue of paintings, pastels, watercolors, and drawings whose sale took place after March 20–21, 1899. Hotel Drouot, Paris. Preface by Arsène Alexandre

Reynold Arnould, *L'œuvre d'Eugène Boudin au Musée des Beaux-Arts du Havre.* Supplement to the catalogue 1952–53, Le Havre, 1955

Charles Sterling and Helene Adhemar, *Musée National du Louvre, Peintures, École française du XIXe siecle,* vol. 1, nos. 121 to 129, Paris, 1958

Jean Dries, *Guide du Musée municipal de Honfleur,* Honfleur, 1959

Eugène Boudin en Bretagne, Musée de Rennes, 1964 (exhibition catalogue)

The Seashore: Paintings of the 19th and 20th Centuries, Carnegie Institute, Pittsburgh, Pennsylvania, 1965 (exhibition catalogue)

Eugène Boudin 1824–1898, Galerie Schmit, Paris, 1965 (exhibition catalogue)

Eugène Boudin 1824–1898, Hirschl & Adler Galleries, Inc., New York, 1966 (exhibition catalogue)

EXHIBITIONS DURING THE ARTIST'S LIFETIME

1850 Le Havre. First exhibition of the Society of the Friends of the Arts (La Société des Amis des Arts)

1852 Le Havre. Biennial exhibition of paintings, sculptures, art objects.

1852 Bordeaux. Third exhibition of the Friends of the Arts of Bordeaux (Les Amis des Arts de Bordeaux)

1853 Bordeaux. Fourth exhibition of the Friends of the Arts of Bordeaux

1856 Rouen. Exhibition

1857 Paris. Musart concert

1858 Le Havre. Society of the Friends of the Arts

1859 From this date on, exhibited regularly at the Salon of French Artists (Le Salon des Artistes Français)

1859 Bordeaux. Eighth exhibition of the Friends of the Arts of Bordeaux

1863 Bordeaux. Twelfth exhibition of the Friends of the Arts of Bordeaux

1864 Bordeaux. Thirteenth exhibition of the Friends of the Arts of Bordeaux

1865 Bordeaux. Fourteenth exhibition of the Friends of the Arts of Bordeaux

1867 World-wide Exhibition of Paris (Exposition Universelle de Paris)

1868 International Maritime Exhibition of Le Havre (Exposition Maritime Internationale du Havre)

1868 Exhibition at Pau

1868 Exhibition at Roubaix

1870 Bordeaux. Nineteenth exhibition of the Friends of the Arts of Bordeaux

1872 Bordeaux. Twentieth Exhibition of the Friends of the Arts of Bordeaux

1874 Bordeaux. Twenty-second Exhibition of the Friends of the Arts of Bordeaux

1874 April 15–May 15. Exhibition of the Cooperative Society of Artists (La Société Anonyme coopera-tive d'Artistes), painters, sculpters, printmakers, etc., organized at the home of the photographer Nadar. (First Impressionist exhibition)

1875 Bordeaux. Twenty-third exhibition of the Friends of the Arts of Bordeaux

1876 Bordeaux. Twenty-fourth exhibition of the Friends of the Arts of Bordeaux

1877 Bordeaux. Twenty-fifth exhibition of the Friends of the Arts of Bordeaux

1878 Bordeaux. Twenty-sixth exhibition of the Friends of the Arts of Bordeaux

1879 Le Havre. Exhibition of the Society of the Friends of the Arts

1880 Le Havre. Exhibition of the Society of the Friends of the Arts

1883 Paris. Galerie Durand-Ruel. Boudin Exhibition

1883 Bordeaux. Exhibition of the Friends of the Arts of Bordeaux

1883 Caen. Regional Competition of 1883. Exhibition of Fine Arts

1884 Bordeaux. Exhibition of the Friends of the Arts of Bordeaux

1885 Le Havre. Exhibition of the Society of the Friends of the Arts

1885 Bordeaux. Exhibition of the Friends of the Arts of Bordeaux

1887 Le Havre. Exhibition of the Society of the Friends of the Arts

1888 Glasgow. Exhibition

1889 Paris. World-wide Exhibition

1889 Paris. Exhibition of the Society of the Fine Arts (founded by the dissidents of the Salon. Meissonier, president)

1889 Bordeaux. Exhibition of the Friends of the Arts of Bordeaux

1889 Paris. Galerie Durand-Ruel. One-man exhibition

1890 Boston. Chase's Gallery

1890 From this date on, exhibited regularly at the Salon of the National Society of Fine Arts (Le Salon de la Société Nationale des Beaux-Arts).

1890 Le Havre. Society of the Friends of the Arts

1891 Paris. Galerie Durand-Ruel. One-man exhibition

1891 Boston. Galerie Durand-Ruel. One-man exhibition

1893 Bordeaux. Forty-first exhibition of the Friends of the Arts of Bordeaux

1896 Le Havre. Exhibition of the Society of the Friends of the Arts

1898 New York. Galerie Durand-Ruel. One-man exhibition

ONE-MAN EXHIBITIONS SINCE 1898

1899 Paris. École Nationale des Beaux-Arts. *Exposition des œuvres d'Eugène Boudin*

1899 Honfleur. Works by Boudin for the Opening of the Musée Saint-Etienne

1900 Paris. Galerie Bernheim-Jeune. *Eugène Boudin*

1903 New York. Durand-Ruel Gallery. *Boudin Exhibition*

1906 Le Havre. Hôtel de Ville. *Retrospective Eugène Boudin*

1908 Paris. Grand Palais. *Retrospective Boudin*

1913 Paris. Galerie Chaine & Simonson. *Tableaux par Eugène Boudin*

1923 Paris. Galerie Durand-Ruel. *Exposition Boudin*

1926 Paris. Galerie Fiquet. *Tableaux d'Eugène Boudin provenant de la collection P.*

1926–27 Paris. Galerie Durand-Ruel. *Tableaux de Boudin*

1929 New York. Durand-Ruel Gallery. *Exhibition of Paintings by Eugène Boudin, 1824–1898*

1931 Paris. Salon d'Automne. *Retrospective Boudin*

1933 New York. Durand-Ruel Gallery. *Exhibition of Paintings by Eugène Boudin, 1824–1898*

1934 London. A. Tooth & Sons. *Boudin Exhibition*

1935–36 Chicago. The Art Institute. *A Loan Exhibition of Paintings by Eugène Boudin*

1937 New York. Durand-Ruel Gallery. *Boudin*

1937 Amsterdam. E. J. Van Wisselingh & Co. *Eugène Boudin*

1938 London. Barbizon House. *Paintings by Eugène Boudin*

1941 Paris. Galerie Élysée. *Les décorations de Boudin pour le château de Bourdainville.*

1941 New York. Durand-Ruel Gallery. *Exhibitions of Paintings by Eugène Boudin*

1945 Paris. Galerie Charpentier. *Retrospective Boudin*

1947 Paris. Galerie Michalon. *Eugène Boudin*

1953 Dieppe. Musée des Beaux-Arts. *Les Boudins du Musée du Havre*

1954 Nice. Musée de Massena. *Eugène Boudin*

1956 Paris. Galerie Katia Granoff. *Les Boudins du Musée Municipal d'Honfleur*

1956 Paris. Galerie Hector Brame. *Eugène Boudin. Peintures, pastels, aquarelles*

1958 Paris. Galerie Charpentier. *100 Paintings by Eugène Boudin*

1958 London. Marlborough Gallery. *Boudin Retrospective Exhibition*

1959 Le Havre. Palais de la Bourse. *Soixante Tableaux par Eugène Boudin*

1962 New York. E. V. Thaw Gallery. *Eugène Boudin*

1964 Rennes. Musée des Beaux-Arts. *Eugène Boudin en Bretagne*

1965 Paris. Galerie Schmit. *Eugène Boudin*

1965 Paris. Musée du Louvre. *Boudin. Aquarelles et pastels*

1966 New York. Hirschl & Adler Galleries. *Eugène Boudin Retrospective Exhibition*

1968 New York. Wally F. Galleries. *Eugène Boudin, Marines and Landscapes*

1974 Paris. Galerie Schmit. *Eugène Boudin, 1824–1898*

GROUP EXHIBITIONS SINCE 1898

1900 Paris. World-wide Exhibition

1903 Paris. Galerie Georges Petit. *Boudin, Jongkind, Pepine, Sisley*

1905 London. Grafton Galleries. *A Selection of Pictures by Boudin, Cezanne, Degas, Manet, Monet, Berthe Morisot, Pissaro, Renoir, Sisley, Exhibited by Durand-Ruel of Paris*

1905 Pittsburgh. Carnegie Institute. *The Impressionists*

1906 London. Leicester Gallery. *E. Boudin and A. Lebourg*

1907 Paris. Galerie des Artistes modernes. *Première Exposition des Artistes Normands*

1909 London. Leicester Galleries. *Exhibition of Paintings by Eugene Boudin and S. Lepine*

1912 Paris. Galerie Bernheim-Jeune. *Eugène Boudin et Janine Aghion*

1912 St. Petersburg. *Exhibition of French Art*

1922 Paris. Galerie Varenne. *Salon des Peintres de la Mer* (Exhibition of Painters of the Sea)

1930 Paris. Galerie Cambacérès. *Paysagistes et peintres de genre. De Deveria à Boudin* (Landscape and genre painters . . .)

1931 Mulhouse. Maison d'art alsacienne. *Boudin, Jongkind, Pissaro*

1934 Honfleur. Musée municipal. *Honfleur et ses Peintres*

1936 London. Alex. Reid & Lefevre. Ltd. *Eugene Boudin and some Contemporaries*

1937   Paris. Galerie des Beaux-Arts. *Naissance de l'Impressionisme* (The Birth of Impressionism)

1942   Paris. Galerie Charpentier. *Le Paysage français de Corot à nos jours* (The French Landscape from Corot to the Present)

1943   New York. Wildenstein & Co. *From Paris to the Sea Down the River Seine*

1945   Paris. Galerie Charpentier. *Paysages de France* (Landscapes of France)

1948   Rouen. *Les peintres normands de Jouvenet à Lebourg* (Normand Painters from Jouvenet to Lebourg)

1949   Bâle. Musée des Beaux-Arts. *Les Impressionistes*

1949–50   London. Royal Academy of Art. *Landscape in French Art*

1951   Paris. Galerie Alfred Daber. *Jongkind, Boudin, marines et paysages* (... seascapes and landscapes)

1952   Saint-Brieuc, Rennes. *La Mer vue par les peintres de Jongkind à nos jours* (The Sea as Seen by Painters from Jongkind to the Present)

1952   Brussels. Palais des Bueax-Arts. *Les Peintres de la Mer et Hommage à Boudin* (The Painters of the Sea and Hommage to Boudin)

1952   Paris. Musée Carnavalet. *Les Chefs d'œuvre des collections parisiennes* (The Masterpieces of Paris Collections)

1953   Honfleur. Société des Artistes Honfleurais. *Boudin, Jongkind, Dubourg*

1953   Paris. Galerie Alfred Daber. *Nature et peinture. Paysages de Corot, Guigou, Boudin, Jongkind, Lepine* (Nature and painting. Landscapes of . . .)

1953   Paris. Musée d'Art Moderne. *De Corot à nos jours au Musée du Havre* (From Corot to the Present at the Museum of Le Havre)

1953   Vancouver. Art Gallery. *French Impressionists*

1955   Paris. Galerie des Beaux-Arts. *Tableaux de collections parisiennes de 1850–1950*

1958   Aix-en-Provance. Galerie Lucien Blanc. *Jongkind, Boudin*

1958   Le Havre. Musée des Beaux-Arts. *Le Havre et les Havrais au XIXe siècle* (Le Havre and the People of Le Havre in the 19th Century)

1959   Paris. Petit Palais. *De Géricault à Matisse. Chefs d'œuvre français des collections privées suisses* (From Gericault to Matisse. French Masterpieces from Private Swiss Collections)

1960   Nice. *Les peintres à Nice et sur la Côte d'Azur* (Painters at Nice and on the Riviera)

1961   Dieppe. Musée des Beaux-Arts. *Les Bains de Mer* (Sea Bathing)

1961   Phoenix. Art Museum. *One Hundred Years of French Painting*

1963   American Federation of Arts. Traveling Exhibition. *The Road to Impressionism*

1964   Albuquerque. University of New Mexico Art Gallery. *Art Since 1889*

1964   Pittsburgh. Carnegie Institute. *The Seashore: Paintings of the 19th and 20th Centuries*

1966   Washington, D.C. National Gallery of Art. *French Paintings from the Collections of Mr. and Mrs. Paul Mellon and Mrs. Mellon Bruce*

1966   Bordeaux. Galerie des Beaux-Arts. *French Paintings in American Collections*

1967   Tulsa. Philbrook Art Center. *French and American Impressionism*

1971   Washington, D.C. Adams Davidson Galleries. *The French Impressionists and Their Followers*

1972   Paris. Galerie Schmit. *Les Impressionists et les Précurseurs*

1974   Bordeaux. Galerie des Beaux-Arts. *Naissance de l'Impressionisme* (The Birth of Impressionism)

1974   Paris. Grand Palais. *Centenaire de l'Impressionisme*

1974   London. Royal Academy of Arts. *Impressionism, its Masters, its Precursors, and its Influence in Britain*